THE LAST HEADLANDS

Poets Published in
The Phoenix Living Poets Series

★

JAMES AITCHISON

ALEXANDER BAIRD · ALAN BOLD

R. H. BOWDEN · FREDERICK BROADIE

GEORGE MACKAY BROWN

HAYDEN CARRUTH · JOHN COTTON

JENNIFER COUROUCLI

GLORIA EVANS DAVIES

PATRIC DICKINSON

TOM EARLEY · D. J. ENRIGHT

IRENE FEKETE

JOHN FULLER · DAVID GILL

PETER GRUFFYDD

J. C. HALL · MOLLY HOLDEN

JOHN HORDER · P. J. KAVANAGH

RICHARD KELL · LAURIE LEE

LAURENCE LERNER

CHRISTOPHER LEVENSON

EDWARD LOWBURY · NORMAN MACCAIG

ROY MCFADDEN

JON MANCHIP WHITE

JAMES MERRILL · RUTH MILLER

LESLIE NORRIS · ROBERT PACK

ARNOLD RATTENBURY

ADRIENNE RICH · JON SILKIN

JON STALLWORTHY

GILLIAN STONEHAM

EDWARD STOREY · TERENCE TILLER

SYDNEY TREMAYNE

LOTTE ZURNDORFER

THE LAST
HEADLANDS

by

DIANA McLOGHLEN

CHATTO AND WINDUS

THE HOGARTH PRESS

1972

Published by
Chatto and Windus Ltd
with The Hogarth Press Ltd
42 William IV Street
London W.C.2

*

Clarke, Irwin & Co. Ltd
Toronto

Distributed in the United States of America
by Wesleyan University Press

ISBN 0 8195 7044 3

ISBN 0 7011 1867 9

© Diana McLoghlen 1972

Printed in Great Britain by
Lewis Reprints Ltd
London and Tonbridge

FOR MY PARENTS
IN MEMORY

Acknowledgement is due to The Irish Times for 'The Last Headlands', 'The Kestrels', 'Orchis', 'The Artist's House at Malahide', 'On the Road', 'The Arbutus', 'Grass of Parnassus', 'The Meadowsweet the Holy Mountain' and 'October Harbour'.

'Poem for India' was published in Manifold.

CONTENTS

THE KESTRELS

The light is brittle, white.
Birch, bird-boned, wild river,
Frost-flower, eddies quiver

In wind and crystal light
Without sweetness or glow,
Muted as ice — till now.

Voices calling high
Beyond the cold hill:
The kestrels mount the sky,

Turning, springing, climbing ever,
Earthward-darting, yet higher still,
A passion of wildness in their cry.

They are the voice of snow-bound river,
Birch, wild light, white frost-flower —
Winter. They speak the hour.

THE ARTIST'S HOUSE AT MALAHIDE

These, the theme of his brush —
Grey and green-white wave, sweep of the sky,
Cloud in a wild bird rush —

Remain, though the hand's clay,
That boarded window a shuttered eye
Cold to the sea-lit day.

Against the gale salt-laden,
Blank as the stone of the grave,
The walls of his garden

On the past close us out:
That lover of sky and wave
Curtained with earth about.

Now when the great
Wings of the winter darken the bay
I come, a century late,

Humble, yet tribal mind,
In the desert homage to pay,
Cast on the wind

Tribute of winter flower;
Cry for a voice to solace the waste in this,
The desolate hour,

Cry, and find no reply —
Only the sweep, the arch of his
Immortal sky.

OCTOBER HARBOUR

So in October one recollects the harbour:
Pale washed stone, thin boats like petals,
Quiet of the evening sky, an iris light
Gentle over the subtle silk of the water.
One calls to mind the curve of the bay, the dark
Trees of landfall, the invader's tower.

Quietude was there by the small, worn harbour,
The men idle under a sky of doves,
Summer at last burnt out and the lightning quenched.
But down by the water's brim a girl's laughter
Floated up from the pebbles, stirred the petals
Scattered a ripple in that air of evening.
As the echo stilled, cold autumn took the harbour.

ON THE ROAD

Today I am travelling through Mayo
God help us; turning
From the sighing of meadowsweet,
The curlew's silver.

Climb now to a strange sky
By thorn, shrunk turves, blenched farms
Angled to the wind's breath,
The edge of the rock that wounds
Poor grass, thin earth.

Mountains veiled lavender
Cloud horizons vague as dream,
The dream too remote for them
Who toiled to harvest a life
From rain and stone.

In the distance lifted
Silver lakes gleam
Like the faraway swords
That never flashed for them.

Today I am travelling through Mayo
Over the high plateau,
Under a vast sky.
Here and there in a silence
Crumbling white stones:

A deserted homestead fallen to die,
Still as the tumbled bones
Of a packhorse that fell by the roadside
And was left to die
While the caravan went on,
Crumpled in the thin grass,
Past cloud and care.

Long since they travelled from Mayo.
Only the long heart-drops,
The crimson fuchsia leaning
To weep for them now.

ORCHIS

A lonely road always, frost and winter
Grip now and quell, while a sunset flare
Lights the harsh hills lilac and lavender.

Yet sudden an image of that pale spring day:
A poor season, the misted air,
The walkers of the same stony way.

In the silence cold spring water welling
By stone and slate, and the far call,
The remote passion of the curlew spilling.

And the thin meadow lit with orchis,
Pale in shadowed sedge by the grey wall —
The sad could fill numb hands with orchis.

Strange, in the frost they rise ghostly here,
Out of time breathing memory.
It is, no doubt, explained somewhere,

Written there in rubrics of stone and water,
Cloud and knotted thorn — calligraphy
The heart as yet cannot decipher.

POEM FOR INDIA

You were never of me, never my country;
In early light you were not even a shadow
On the clear morning, a legend of summer.
Before thought's prick you were unknown
As the Bear at midnight. When from a flurry
Of wires, lacerating letters, trains,
Pale in tussore Aunt Alice entered,
For the first time the syllables "India" fell,
Chiming around her. She came a wraith,
A rose about to fall, the petals scattered,
Irrevocable. A summer, a day,
She lay in the wicker chair under the flowering
Syringa boughs; she was whiter than they.
It was India had drained her colour, the great
Tiger of the heat had leapt at her heart.
She smiled and gave us her topee to play with,
Told us of elephants, left a devastating
Gentleness on the air when she went away,
Further than India, beyond all tigers.

And you, India, receded again.

There were, of course, later impersonal
Flashes of gold, the fanfares of history,
Letters and tales. Neighbours journeyed, wrote
Of the plains, hill stations, a marigold sky,.
The haunting psalm of the sad wide waters,
Mute sands — returned with only the phrase
"When we were in India" a label against
A final merging in the local mould.

Later still — a bedsitter in Kensington,
A tall, quiet house in the quiet square,
An attic, a window, the waves of trees
Whispering, lime-green in the lamplight, all night.
Spanish students and impecunious

15

Typists climbed up and down ceaselessly
The long, high staircase, not knowing each other.

Met perhaps in the kitchen basement
At evening's table, the lambent air
Warm as cinnamon, the singing fire.
And the quiet, dark, scrupulous hands
Placed bowls of rice, brought saffron curry;
A lamp of honey, an amber rug falling
Over the door, against the night and London.

Recollect a murmur in the dark, a stir,
An hour of hidden festival,
The daughter of the house, her guests gazelles
Glimpsed from a fog-encircled stair.
The Kensington night opened in flower,
Blossomed in saris and sandalwood,
Fireflies alight in the cave of the hall,
A moment of flame — and the fog returned.

You recede now before the searing
Image of famine, the pleas outstretched
Shaming the west. Yes, one would forget
You, India. The voices turn, pass by.
Yet here, among the towering trees of sunset
In the still garden half ruinous
Planted in memory of an Indian hour
By the sad traveller retreating westward for ever,
I walk under the boughs of a legend, see
The stars of the Southern Cross as petals falling.
They lie along the branches, the eternal snows,
The waxen blossoms with the hearts of silence.
Wide scarlet flowers, silken as saris, flare,
The falls of light, the great bells tolling
For the Himalayas, Kashmir, Nepal.
I walk in the shadow of giants, knowing
Only the leaves gentle on the evening wind.
I see the leaves are dark as the quiet hands.

THE LODDEN LILY

Tread these still verges
Between spring and winter,
By ooze of the marsh
And silent river,
The empurpled alder.

Bleached tattered pennants,
The long ago reeds
Drape winter's black stream.
In Ash Wednesday fields
Ewes are grey cloud.

Crevice and rockfall
The white hills blue-vein,
Faint on the wind
The powder of snow,
The hazel pollen.

In the wind's hush now
Between hawk and lamb cry,
Green-tipped in ice
The Lodden lily
By the river is risen,

Poised, still and slender.
Look long, and withdraw.
But in the blue dusk return,
Search the frail spinney,
The lily has gone —

Slipped away as it came
To the river and legend.
Yet a leaf shall remain,
A lance to tilt
At Time's heart of stone.

B

A LEGACY

Remembering under these trees of summer,
Remembering a year ago my coming
In from the sunlit, glittering globe,
The heart of the green garden blowing,
To find you very quiet among your books,
The pipe between your fingers fallen cold,
Gazing abstracted at a sky
Of kingcups over the western trees.
Careless, I asked you, daughterwise, your thoughts.
"I was thinking then" slowly you said "of Greer".
"Why, Colonel Greer, you've heard me speak of him.
One of the nicest men that ever walked."
"But he — ?" "Killed this day, fifty odd years ago.
He and Captain Synge on the same day
In that one dreadful battle." And I knew
The memory was closer than the trees,
The trees of summer round our two lives sighing.
You called down the long whispering of the leaves
To the old ghosts, the Guards rising in shadow
On the sad Salient. "And it was summer,
Long days and the long march, and villages,
Paeonies, a veiled grey church in columbines,
And ruined scarlet poppies, while the guns
Called us ahead, tolled for the falling light,
A generation moving to the dark."

And come this summer you are gone,
Withdrawn even beyond your memories.

And now to me bequeathed a stranger June
Leafy with rainy sounds and presages,
Now alerted to the bugle call
The sudden recognition of a date,
Lone keeper of an anniversary.

Knowing the far and indefinable
Sadness falling from the kingcup sky.

You have willed me a testament of names
That twine about my garden thoughts in thorns —
The Menin Road — the Birr Crossroads — and Ypres.
They stir in the dark petals of my summer.
Now rises there in every leaf a lance,
And all my lovely proud and scarlet flowers
With new intent under the sunset burn.

THE SMALL TRIANGULAR FIELDS

It is the small
Triangular fields beneath the rain,
The hungry buttercups that lean
To a dark wind

That haunt the thought
In this outmoded neighbourhood, a land
Of disused mine, the leaderless shaft
And worked out seam.

They wait in small
Angular houses, fading terraces.
An echoing stair mounts perpendicular,
Alleys are stone,

Small windows veiled.
Time has ebbed from the long street, the steps
Of prosperity gone. These sons
Of exile know

All things pass,
The tilt of the wave and the long slump to the hollow.
They are too proud to unlock a bitterness,
An apportioned pain.

One must not stir
The calm, their detached courtesy,
Nor peer to see what past is shut within
The narrow frame

In the dresser's hold.
One does not enquire as to what they are waiting for.
The darkening buttercups passionate lean
Into the rain.

THE HAPPY PLACE

It was a happy place, I saw as I came
There in the gentle day under the white
Light of the river, the blowing cloud and the white
Light of the May. And the flow of the wind
Over the chiming fields and young bright grasses
In the quiet of the lace-white street was one
With the swallow's flight up the irised river
Where I paused by the bridge in the noon.
The door of the church stood wide
To the fields and airs, the children and the voices.
And the winds, the children drifted through.
Shadow of wings on a sill, the white of the May.

And I suddenly saw how they who came
From the wind-wreathed townland of chiming voices
Unknowing went to a world of iron,
To an hour of steel and the stranger's chill
Indifference. They would know
No weapons against that night. And there
I could have wept in the sunlit May
For the pity of it, for those who had gone
Unarmed. But I would not stain with a tear
That innocent sun, nor daub with my dark
Of pity the grace of a place that owned
Nothing but happiness under the white
Light of the river falling from stone to stone.

GRASS OF PARNASSUS

It was a good summer: your neighbours,
Or, rather your old neighbours' sons
Reaped, got their hay.

The land did well. And why
Wouldn't it after the grand weather?
There is meal now

In the chest against the winter,
Turf for the long
Dark without stars.

The Hogans' cattle are sleek. But the horns
Of the vagrants scorned in their passing
At random grazed

Your pastures, pushing through hazels
And thorns of the boreen. The Quinns'
Barn is full.

In your long meadow only brown bees
Move, gathering a stranger honey from pale
Small lilac flowers.

I walk your grey avenue under
The pines whisht in their sighing,
The heart of noon

Golden and still, September
Gentle and misted on the far Slieve Bloom,
The bogland amber.

It is the doves' voice in your rooftree's ruin
Weaving content. That rose she planted
Has climbed to the sky,

Leaf on light. Who am I to come
With my sorrow, the only one
To this quiet ground?

Here is no crying. The fields are sunlit.
In the empty horse park where you and Con
Ran in a young joy

Butterflies rising lilt before me
Through the falls of the grass. I walk
Where you, a boy,

Turned to follow a rushlight vision,
The wing of a shy muse slipping
Through a haunted land.

They have carried their harvest, the neighbours.
Here there are small white flowers
That spring at footfall.

The ancients' holy and delicate Grass
Of Parnassus, mark of the muse,
Has sealed with stars

Your wild yet gentle land. By sedge and stone
Your land is aflower. I write this
For you. And Con.

THE LAST HEADLANDS

Climb to the last headlands,
The recognition
Of wind and ocean.

A kingly Atlantic, twelve
Visionary peaks, a sky
Superb with summer.

Acknowledge now the end
Of the known world, the old
Outworn, outcropped land.

Under the wind small flowers
Purple darker than essence
Of the dark Atlantic.

Small, still gentians
Darken the bright grasses
By the harsh wave's fall.

They are the last flowers
Of the old world: beyond
Their petals America

Lies, the sad forest;
Beyond the last calyx
Massachusetts and Michigan.

Flowers quieter than dusk,
Quieter than wavefall, knowing
Only the salt on the wind,

Beyond them only the long
Wave and the long heartache,
A long creed dying.

THE HAWK IN AUTUMN

High in an air of fine-spun amber,
The hour stilled in a crystal gyre,
The red hawk hovers in a golden spiral,
Poised to survey his autumn kingdom.
Now is our October
Mirrored in that round, implacable eye:
The gilded birch and dewberry moor,
Wide sombre slopes of the bracken turning,
And the river bearing the last of the summer,
The last of passion in the great woods burning —
All now reduced to one common
Passionless denominator
Reflected in a jewelled, pitiless eye.

And that most delicate precision
Instrument, the hawk's heart chiming,
Suspended on the spinning spokes of the wind,
Armoured against the iron-clad weather,
The volleyed hail and the north wind's knife,
By the tenderest deeps of downy feather.
Can that steeled heart and flint-edged mind
Continue the spiral's consummation
Untarnished always by doubt and fear?

May the red hawk then remain unknowing
Of a desert beyond the wastes of winter,
Unsuspecting an assailant bolder,
The ultimate fall, a chasm deeper
Than the river's plunge, an abyss colder
Than the tooth of the ice
Or the mountain's shadow.

THE MEADOWSWEET THE HOLY MOUNTAIN

Beyond the meadowsweet, the holy mountain,
Holy Croagh Patrick rises, transcending legend,
Veiled in a far sunset, the flame from the skies.

Mile on vagrant mile, the meadowsweet wanders,
The long quiet of pool and sky to inherit.
Likewise the pilgrims journey through the evening land.

Stone and silvery water, the earth and air
Dissolve in sweetness, lulling the darkening curlew
On the lonely bog consumed in a dying fire.

Pilgrim, is this your foretaste of Paradise:
The flowering waters sweet in the summer wild?
The traveller remarks agreeably the fine

Spirea ulmaria of the bogland parts.
Blown down time to shadow an alien sun
It is the anguish numbs and for ever the heart.

Under the holy mountain all are one.

THE SUMMER IN FRIZINGTON ROAD

Now summer has come to a long street the swifts
Swoop and sweep on scimitar wings.

Now sightless walls are warm, and the sun
Almost has drilled to the core of the dark

Through cold seeped stone to the small
Back kitchen and narrow stair.

Forgotten the boarded rubble mopes to the sky.
While the women carved in clusters lean at the door,

Or talk in the street. And time is mild in the sun.

Hunched Red-Indian-wise on haunches, the men
Gather by hollowed steps, limp hands
Tormented no more by pick or pulley, and watch
Their daughters' sons in the street's brief summer.

It is as pleasant a place as any;
So be it there is no fall of the past
To bury all from the day, and the wick
Of subterranean anguish flare.

Walk quietly now in the sun, nor glance
At sightless walls, the bricked-up, boarded things.

Grandchildren over-confident call,
Sweetwilliams crimson dark on the windowsill,

Now summer has come to the long street and the swifts
Sweep and soar on their undefeated wings.

HUTTON ROOF

I think we shall come soon
Beyond the sleep of meadows,
Out of these small green
Valleys of history,

Quit the reiteration
Of lintel and corbel,
Eaves secretive and laden,
Viola and apple,

And go back to the beginning,
Back beyond reaping and sowing,
Further than the Plantagenets,
Further than Boadicea dying,

To the thin air and the old rock,
The long bones unstirred by larksong
Cold under the blue of summer,
And the darkened hearthstone.

We climb now to hills
That rise silent shoulder to shoulder
To the skies of summer, hills
Azure and fainter than harebells.

I think that when we come
To the hills' roof we shall find
That perhaps for which
We have been searching always.

We hear the tongues of the oaks:
We mount to the wind
Flowing from the rock. And still,
Always we climb.

INSCRIPTION FOR A CHINESE BELL

Eleven months of the patchwork year
Cold the bell as stone on the cold stone sill.
The calendar stirs no more than the whirr
Of the jangled clock aloft, while few heed still
The tablet proclaiming white as Martinmas ice
In eighteen-forty-one a victory
At the Chinese fort where the sunset waters flow,
The Captain mournfully paying glory's price,
To whom this stone is raised as monument now
By his sorrowing widow in pious memory.

And the captured bell, lethal and grim as lead,
Blank and withdrawn, iron become stone,
The proud, secretive script unread
A century, remote, untouched by all
Pied country rites and straw-decked pageantry —
Carols and brides, the pumpkin festival —
Darkens lifeless in captivity,
A seaflung shell, the wave and colour gone.

Yet when lent lilies grace on grace unfold,
On some late afternoon of April's gold,
Winds gentle from a daffodil sky,
A long beam through the narrow window falls,
Strikes like a gong the bronze, the golden bell
Until the rubrics swinging tell,
Plangent under April light,
Of winds and temples in the Western Hills,
The silence flowering where the emperors lie,
Torches of lilac lifted in the night;

Dragons and gongs, letters and overtones,
Letters such as the grave Captain penned
To England, read on daisy-ribboned lawns,
Caged in the basketry of chairs and trees —

Wide eyes as velvet as auriculas —
Letters and voices fluttering the breeze
Among the muslins and the primulas.

Till it blows, darkens, and the rising gale
Whirls the dragons and smoke, the storm-dyed crowds
Beyond the reach of the day. A ship sets sail
Westward bound, into the mist and clouds
Quenching the April light. And the church is cold,
The gold is lead, the colour of rain, and numb.
The cold spring rain slants on the yew-dark mould.
The great iron bell is fallen still, is dumb.

SPEAKING OF MR. PHINN

I do not know,
Although he speaks often of past years, past seas,
Referring dispassionately
To winters of great torment
And tempest-bedevilled voyages,
Yet still I do not know
What great wave it was
Bore him on a crest of chance
And retreating in a long
Empty withdrawal
Over shingles of ill-luck,
Left him stranded here
In this quite exceptionally
Unlovely town,
Risen once to the black wand of coal
And surviving, rather surprisingly,
With a grim and terrier determination
The long tip of the Depression,
Emerged from "Hitler's War"
(As distinct from a private, personal war)
To move, still grimly,
Into the neon flash of the 1960's.

But you will not find Mr. Phinn
Walking the long black terraces of the east wind
By Jubilee Villas or Keir Hardie Prospect,
Nor becalmed in the market-place
With the great-chinned women
In their headscarves and raincoats,
Their eyes expressionless guarding
Any glimmer of a heart's glow
That was not dowsed in the long slump,
While they compare the bright
Candyfloss of the market
With the red labels of the Co-op.

31

Nor will you see Mr. Phinn
Where the rain spatters the Legion's hall
And the puddles flicker by the gravel
On the stillborn new estate.
No. You must turn aside from the windy town,
Push open a faded door,
Heavy as if someone inside
Were leaning against it, but there
Is no one, only a passage,
A chilly mirror reflecting the few
Inconsequential coats and caps,
And down the darkness to another door,
Which, opened in some
Trepidation, discloses
A square cold window, a square bleached table,
A flaccid rag rug, and Mr. Phinn
Cabined in a corner seat
By the poppied glow in a large black range
Armoured and fortified with knobs and bars.
His bald head bent, he is drawing
On small neat squares of paper
Moonflowers and Chinese birds
Such as are not seen
In these parts, but Mr. Phinn
Knows all seas, all latitudes.

Now, peering over
Small round spectacles,
He rises cheerily,
Moving carefully, a little bent,
Tacitly inclining to years and weather,
"Well! Well! What wind! What rain!
Last night! Did you hear the storm?
But then we cannot look
For anything better.
Not until we have come
Safe past January" —

Or February. Or whatever —
"Oh no! We sailors used to say
We could not count to have come
Through until we had rounded
This month. Ah! I've seen
Some terrible seas this day".
So Mr. Phinn philosopher
Not looking for anything better,
Tightens the bolts and bars
On the four-square range,
Hears unperturbed the wind
Roar in the rigging of the chimneys
And rattling T.V. aerials,
Glances with a professional eye
At the storm clouds scudding
Beyond the cold grey window,
And resumes his brush and paper,
Colouring with the gold of sunflowers
A bird from the Indian Ocean
Or painting, most delicately,
One perfect and sea-blue rose.

Perhaps these days he rises
A little more slowly,
Moves with more difficulty
Across the creaking deck of the kitchen floor;—
Peers in some perplexity
From the look-out of the landing window,
As if he were not quite sure
Of the compass holding steady.
While the cold sea fog
Muffles Keir Hardie Prospect,
Blurs the concrete of William Morris Place,
Presses nearer, silently,
Down Corporation Avenue —
The black fog colder than frost.

Some day I think I shall come
To find a great shining wave has swept
In and borne him away,
This time to an uncharted sea.

EPITAPH FOR A SEASIDE TERRACE

Fifty, sixty years ago
Such pride dwelt here, the lions of stone
Surveyed serene their just domain
And turned undoubting eyes upon
The eastern waves, as if in scorn
Of the sunset hills, the mist, the rain
And all the storms the west might blow.
Who in this terrace pondered then
The mightier one — stone lion or time?
Imperial pride or western clime?

But now who peer, ghosts or men,
Stirred as a drifting seabird calls,
From their lace-shrouded shabbiness
At the world beyond these flaking walls,
Find in the tangled greenery
The lions grown blurred and featureless,
The foghorn mournful out to sea,
The long, slow drops of crimson flowers
The fuchsia dripping hour on hours
In the gardens damp and desolate.
Yes, fallen now their high estate.
All glory dead as yesteryear,
The stone lions vanquished one by one.
All's finished now and all's undone —
West wind and rain are masters here.

THE WILD SWANS

Solitary under December light,
Through the fronds of the frost, the still
Spell of the rime

I have heard the aerial voices
And seen in the first white of the morning sky
The wild swans flying

Outstretched in a long grace on the cold of the air,
Into the heart of the pale sky intent
On paler wings.

All day I am haunted by that image of dawn
Amid inconsequential
Or ponderous things

Recurring to stir to an old delight and awe
At moons and wonders unveiled.
And yet I know

It was the pulse of flight on the currents of wind,
It was only the wild birds flying
In the lee of the snow.

O my forgotten peoples — you Molloys,
O'Driscolls, Quinns!
I see you now

Risen tall against a dawn
Paler than this, colder,
Remoter, out of
Very early time.

Pushing aside the long dark you come
Into the faint and legendary light

Over withdrawn

White waters and stiff, muted sedge,
The bogland silent under the rime's
Alien breath,

To hear, as I, the throb and passage of wings,
An unknown clan, a strangeness
In the air,

The surge of feathers through frost, a sky
Of ice, and voices
Falling far.

And watched them pale beyond the paling star,
Beyond the rim of the bog, beyond the blind
Disc of the light.

So would you under the eaves of night
By the last embers' glow recall
The great wings of the dawn.

In the wind's creak, the light of your dying fire,
Relate the vision in the white skies, tell
Of the children of Lir.

IMAGES

You said that we should hold in days like these
To certain recollections of certain men's
Unswerving thought, to places and images

Of splendour and outmoded pride.
So I would recall that seaboard town
Lit by the flaunting flood of a peacock tide,

But would turn from the sails and clamorous quay
To a grey cluster of steps and doors,
Those houses drawn aside from the century,

Cold until evening touched with flame and flare
Fanlight and wall, and ancient down ancient roads
The tall queens came in shawls to take the air.

Remember that great rowan tree that stood
Over Wine Street in scarlet glory leaning,
Flinging to frigid stone a fruit like blood.

Recall the darkness and the wind that stormed
In from the Atlantic, beating at roof and mind
All night till nothing seemed but could be harmed

By that wild force. But when the dawn
Came cold and blue up from the heaving quay
The voices rang triumphant from the stone.

"A grand morning, Glory be!" It is
Such images you would have me hold as you
Hoarded thoughts against a time like this.

THE ARBUTUS

(For my Mother)

I have forgotten almost
The pale sugar flowers in panicles fainter
Than the light of a lost

Happiness falling,
The faint drowned bell of the foghorn to sea
On the salt mist tolling.

Now I remember
Only the lamps of the crimson fruit marking
The paths of November.

Rich in the white
Of the fog that hung cold on the walls by the sea,
Their lanterns were bright

Steadfast in burning
As the hearth of a heart, the long beam through the night
Of the lightship turning.

But the petals are dying.
The footsteps echo like rain through the branches
In the stormbird's crying

To what cold new venture
Out on the searoads, beyond the lamps' warning,
To the years of the stranger.

Still shall the arbutus
Hear the November wavefall, the drowned bell
Out to sea, the far voices

On the sea path . . . . . . But no.
Deep in a heart fainter than the petals
Of the wax flower I know

The long mists rolled in.
The great tide of the years quenched the lamps long ago.
Too late shall I turn;

The landmarks are gone.
Crumbled the long walls where the white fog hung cold.
The arbutus is down.